PIANO · VOCAL · GUITAR

BIG BOOK of LATIN AMERICAN SONGS

This publication is not for sale in
the E.C. and/or Australia
or New Zealand.

ISBN 0-7935-1383-9

HAL·LEONARD CORPORATION

7777 W. BLUEMOUND RD. P.O. BOX 13819 MILWAUKEE, WI 53213

BIG BOOK of LATIN AMERICAN SONGS

A ÉSA

Words and Music by MANUEL ALEJANDRO
and MARIA ALEJANDRA

é - sa, __ la he que - ri - do yo a ra - biar, __

la he que - ri - do yo a mo - rir. ___ ¡Tú no

Additional Lyrics

2. A ésa,
   Que ahora está, como ya ves
   Destruída de rodar,
   Yo le he escrito mil poemas
   A sus ojos y a su piel.
   To Chorus

3. A ésa,
   Le he enseñado a besar,
   A sentir, y a ser mujer,
   Y ya ves que aventajada.
   ¡Quién se lo iba a suponer!
   To Chorus

ADELITA

English Lyric by
OLGA PAUL

English Lyric by OLGA PAUL
Arranged by RICARDO ROMERO

A FELICIDADE

Words by VINICIUS DE MORALES
Music by ANTONIO CARLOS JOBIM

ADIOS MUCHACHOS

AMAPOLA
(PRETTY LITTLE POPPY)

By JOSEPH M. LACALLE
New English Words by ALBERT GAMSE

THE BREEZE AND I

Words by AL STILLMAN
Music by ERNESTO LECUONA

CARIOCA

Words by GUS KAHN and EDWARD ELISCU
Music by VINCENT YOUMANS

Rhythmically

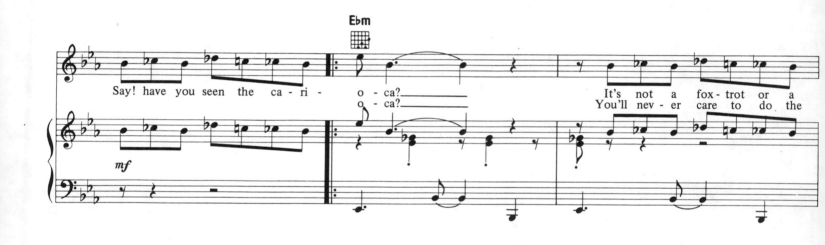

Say! have you seen the ca - ri - o - ca?_____ It's not a fox - trot or a
o - ca?_____ You'll nev - er care to do the

pol - ka,_____ It has a lit - tle bit of new rhy - thm, a
pol - ka,_____ And then you re - al - ize the blue hu - la and

CASTIGAME

Words and Music by RAFAEL P. BOTIJA,
AENRI QUETA and RAMOS NUNEZ

¿Qué es lo que me pa-sa es-ta no - che,
¿Quién se-rás que no te co-noz - co?

que dor-mir no pu-de, be-bé?
Co-mo ha-brás lle-ga-do has-ta mi?

Pa-ra con-fun-dir de tus la - bios,   su po-der
¿Co-mo he de po-der de-tec-tar - te,   y de-jar-

24

Additional Lyrics

Verse 3:
¿Qué es lo que me pasa esta noche?
¿Qué locura me hizo caer?
Hasta permitir que me lleves,
Com un barco de papel.

Verse 4:
¿Quién seras que todo lo vences,
Y haces lo que quieres de mi?
¿Cómo habra podido entregarme,
Simplemente por decir?

Bridge 2:
Mañana yo me haré por supuesto,
Al verme pensaré. ¿Cómo pude ser de esto?
To Chorus

CHEGA DE SAUDADE
(NO MORE BLUES)

Words by VINICIUS DE MORAES
Music by ANTONIO CARLOS JOBIM
English Lyrics by JON HENDRICKS & JESSIE CAVANAUGH

No more blues, I'm
Vai mi - nha tris -

goin' back home. No, no more
te - za E diz a e-

3. Dentro dos meus braços,   Que é prá acabar
   Os abraco hão de ser   com êsse negocio
   Milhões de abraços,   de viver longe de mim,
   Apertado assim,   Não quero mais esse negócio
   Colado assim,   De você viver assim,
   Colado assim,   Vamos deixar dêsse negócio
   Abraços e beijinhos   De você viver sem mim,
   E carinhos sem ter fim,   Não quero mais êsse negócio
                                De viver longe de mim.

CHERRY PINK AND
APPLE BLOSSOM WHITE

French Words by JACQUES LARUE
English Words by MACK DAVID
Music by LOUIGUY

CHIAPANECAS
(WHILE THERE'S MUSIC THERE'S ROMANCE)

English Lyric by ALBERT GAMSE
Spanish Lyric by EMILIO DE TORRE
Arranged by RICARDO ROMERO

Un cla-vel cor-té___ Por la sie-rra fui___ ca-mi - ni-to de___
*While there's mu-sic sweet,_ With a rhyth-mic beat_ and a mel - o-dy_*

__ mi ran-cho___ Co-mo el vien-to fué___ mi ca-ba-llo fiel___
*__ ro - man-tic,___ Let me dance with you,_ Till the night is thru_*

__ à lle-var-me has-ta___ su la-do. Lin - da flor de a-bril___
__While there's mu-sic there's___ ro - mance.___ 'Round and 'round we'll glide,_

CINCO ROBLES
(FIVE OAKS)

Lyric by
LARRY SULLIVAN

Words by LARRY SULLIVAN
Music by DOROTHY WRIGHT

Moderate waltz

CLAVELITOS
(CARNATIONS)

English Lyrics by
MARJORIE HARPER

Music and Spanish Lyrics by
ESTIC and J. VALVERDE

Buy car - na - tions! _____ Who would like a car - na - tion? _____
Cla - ve - li - tos. _____ a quien le doy cla - ve - les!

_____ Buy car - na - tions! _____ Fair - est flow'r of cre - a - tion! _____
Cla - ve - li - tos. _____ Pa - ra los chu - rum - be - les!

_____ My car - na - tions! _____ Here is one that I've got just for you!
Cla - ve - li - tos. _____ Que los doy con los o - jos ce - raos,

For I use them my love to re-veal; With them man-y a heart I can steal!
Por-que tie-ne mu chis-mo quin-qué! pa ro-bar co-ra-zo-nes o-lé!
But to one I a-dore Goes the best of my store With the love that I
Yen-se-nar-les la e-sen-cia pre-sen-cia y po-ten-cia que ya sa-be us-
feel! Dear, I am wait-ing to hear if your heart is mine, If my car-na-tions helped
té! Si tu me quie-res mi ni-no ca-ri-no Yo te da-ré un cla-ve-
bring you to me! Oh! If we should mar-ry, Where-ev-er we tar-ry, Think
li-to bo-ni-to. Y ve-ras que bien mar-cha-mos si es ta-mos

44

CORAZON CORAZON

Words and Music by
JOSE MA. NAPOLEON

CODA

zón.   Co - ra - zón.   Has-ta el úl - ti-mo la - ti - do, co - ra -

zón.   Co - ra - zón,   co - ra - zón.   Es-ta-

Repeat and Fade

ré siem-pre con - ti - go, co - ra - zón.   Co - ra -

Additional Lyrics

2. Donde vayas he de ir contigo, amor.
   Si una mano necesitas dos tendré,
   Y si sufres una pena,
   Una pena sufriré.
   Cuando rías a tu lado reiré.
   To Chorus

3. Cuando nos quedemos solos otra vez,
   Porque tengan nuestros hijios que crecer.
   Tal vez yo te invite al cine.
   Y en lo oscuro como ayer,
   Algun beso en la mejilla te daré.
   To Chorus

THE COFFEE SONG
(THEY'VE GOT AN AWFUL LOT OF COFFEE IN BRAZIL)

Words and Music by BOB HILLIARD
and DICK MILES

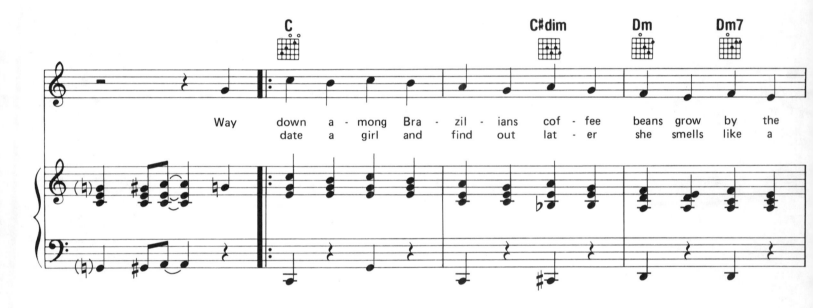

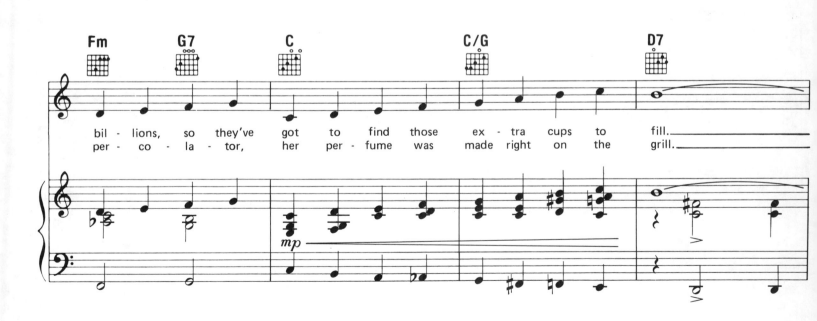

CUBAN LULLABY

Words and Music by DON ALVAREZ
and MARION SUNSHINE

Ev - 'ry time you hold me to your heart

'neath this love - ly Cu - ban moon,

I can feel a thrill with - in me start

CUMANA

Words by HAROLD SPINA & ROC HILLMAN
Music by BARCLAY ALLEN

CUBAN PETE

By JOSÉ NORMAN

EL RELICARIO

Un dia de San Eu - ge - nio yen-do ha cia el Pra - do le co-no-

Wind swirled a - long the high - way when first we met, I re - mem - ber

Additional Lyrics

2. Wind blew on the arena when first we met, I remember yet,
   Your fight was brave to see, but fear was over me,
   Wind was your enemy my Toreador!
   Your cape up-flying, I saw you lying,
   I saw you dying, My Matador.
   Then in your dark eyes so deep and tender,
   I seemed to recognize, Love's surrender,
   and your last greeting, gently enteating,
   Set my heart beating, as you said low:
   To Chorus

2. Era un Lunes Abrileño el toreaba y a verle fui.
   Nunca lo hi cierra que a quella tarde,
   De sentimien to crei morir.
   Al dar un lance, Cayó en la arena,
   Se sintióherido, Miró haciami.
   Y un Relicario sacó del pecha,
   Que yo enseguidu reconoci,
   Cuando el Torero, caia inerte,
   En su delirio decia asi:
   To Chorus

DESAFINADO
(SLIGHTLY OUT OF TUNE)

English Words by JON HENDRICKS & JESSIE CAVANAUGH
Original Words by NEWTON MENDONCA
Music by ANTONIO CARLOS JOBIM

DINDI

Music by ANTONIO CARLOS JOBIM
Portuguese Lyrics by ALOYSIO de OLIVEIRA
English Lyrics by RAY GILBERT

DON'T CRY FOR ME ARGENTINA

(From The Opera "EVITA")

Lyric by TIM RICE
Music by ANDREW LLOYD WEBBER

It won't be ea-sy, you'll think it strange When I

EL RANCHO GRANDE (ALLA EN)
(MY RANCH)

English Lyrics by
BARTLEY COSTELLO

Tune Uke
G C E A

English Lyrics by BARTLEY COSTELLO
Spanish Lyrics & Music by SILVANO R. RAMOS

I love to roam out yon - der, Out where the Buf - f'lo
A - llá en el ran - cho gran - de, A - llá don - de vi -

wan - der, _____ Free as the Eag - le fly - ing, I'm
vi - a, _____ Ha - bía u - na ran - che ri - ta Que a -

*) Symbols are for Banjo or Guitar

rop-ing and a-ty-ing, I'm rop-ing and a-ty-ing. _____
le-gre me de - ci - a, Que a-le-gre me de - ci - a. _____

rit. _____

VERSE

Give me my ranch and my cat-tle, _____
Give me my bri - dle and sad-dle, _____
Te voy ha - cer tus cal - zo - nes, _____

_____ Far from the great cit - y's rat-tle; _____
_____ And my old Pin - to I'll strad-dle; _____
_____ *Co - mo los u - sa el ran - che - ro;* _____

C7

Give me a big herd to bat - tle, _____ For I just
I'll get the cow - boys a - rid - ing, _____ Out where the
Te los co - mien - - zo de la - na, _____ Te los a -

F

love herd - ing cat - tle.
rust - - lers are hi - ding.
ca - - bo de cue - ro.

D.S.

Fine

D.S.
varias veces

3rd Verse

Some-times the winter storms tearing,
Set all the cattle a-raring,
But when the winter is over,
We're sure enough in the clover.

Nunca te fies de promesas
Ni mucho menos de amores
Que si te dan calabzas
Verás lo que son ardores.

4th Verse

Give me the wide open spaces,
That's just where I know my place is,
I love the Ro-de-o dearly,
And the Big Round-Up yearly.

Pon muy atento el oído
Cuando rechine la puerta
Hay muertos que no hacen ruido
Y son muy gordas sus penas.

5th Verse

Tho' we play seven eleven,
My Ranch is next door to Heaven,
We smile when we take a beatin',
But hang a rat when he's cheatin'.

Cuando te pidan cigarro
No des cigarro y cerillo
Porque si das las dos cosas
Te tantearán de zorrillo.

FEELINGS

(¿DIME?)

English Words and Music by MORRIS ALBERT
Spanish Lyric by THOMAS FUNDORA

89

ESA TRISTE GUITARRA

Words and Music by MANUEL ALEJANDRO
and ANA MAGDALENA

1. Si ves u - na flor __
2. A - quel go - rri - on __
3.-4. *See additional lyrics*

__ mar - chi - ta - da en el sue __ lo,
__ que sus - pi - ra en el ár - bol,

91

Additional Lyrics

3. Si un dia la lluvia acaricia tu cuerpo,
   No es agua, mi amor, son tan solo mis besos.

4. Si el sol en la calle calienta tu cara,
   Son rayos de amor que me salen del alma.
   To Bridge

ESPAÑA CANI
(Paso Doble)

By PASCUAL MARQUINA

ESTOY SENTADO AQUI

By CESAR ROSAS

Es - toy ___ sen - ta - do a - qui,

que me pa - sen la te - qui - la, el a - mor y tris - te vi - da no me im - por - ta a

THE FACE I LOVE

Lyric by RAY GILBERT
Music by MARCOS VALLE
Portugese Lyric by PAULO VALLE and G. PINGARILNO

FLAMINGO

Lyrics by ED ANDERSON
Music by TED GROUYA

THE GIRL FROM IPANEMA
(GAROTA DE IPANEMA)

Original Words by VINICIUS DE MORAES
English Words by NORMAN GIMBEL
Music by ANTONIO CARLOS JOBIM

MCA music publishing

A GAY RANCHERO

Words by ABE TUVIM and FRANCIA LUBAN
Music by J.J. ESPINOSA

A ___ gay ran -
Va ___ mos a

cher - o,
Te - pa

a ___ cab - al - ler - o
tie - rra so - ña - da

can ___ al - ways
don - de la

Additional Lyrics

2. Back on his rancho, we now find Pancho
With his pepita by his side.
She thinks he's handsome, worth any ransom,
To him she's still the blushing bride.
Our Gay Ranchero, our caballero,
Still tells the world of how they met.
This Gay Ranchero, this caballero,
Says he has nothing to regret.
Now to end the story that I once was told
Here's a little secret that I must unfold
For they found the promise that they had in store.
Now they're really counting chicos by the score.

2. En el potrero de los maizales
tengo un pedazo de jardín
como lo riego todas las tardes
ya dió botones el jazmín
Así, le pasa a mi virgencita
cuando le doy todo mi amor
ya le a nacido la florecita
que le robé del corazón
Que lindas las mañanas cuando sale el sol
a si son las Alteñas de este alrededor.
Alegres y bonitas todo el tiempo estan
las lindas Altenitas de Tepati tlan.

THE GIFT!
(RECADO BOSSA NOVA)

English Words by PAUL FRANCIS WEBSTE[R]
Original Words and Music by DJALMA FERREIRA and LUIZ ANTONIO

GITANERIAS

Transcription by
LOUIS SUGARMAN

By ERNESTO LECOUNA

GUANTANAMERA

Original Lyrics and Music by JOSE FERNANDEZ DIAS (JOSEITO FERNANDEZ)
Music adaptation by PETE SEEGER
Lyric adaptation by HECTOR ANGULO, based on a poem by JOSE MARTI

Spanish verses

1. Yo soy un hombre sincero,
   De donde crece la palma,
   Y antes de morirme quiero,
   Echar mis versos del alma.

2. Mi verso es de un verde claro,
   Y de un carmin encendido,
   Mi verso es un cierro herido,
   Que busca en el monte amparo.

3. Con los pobres de la tierra,
   Quiero yo mi suerte echar,
   El arroyo de la sierra,
   Me complace mas que el mar.

NOTE - Repeat chorus after
each of the above verses.

Literal translation

Guantanamera: A lady
of Guantanamo
Guajira: Young woman

I'm a sincere man from
the land of palms. Before
dying, I wish to pour forth
the poems of my soul.

My verses are soft green but
also a flaming red. My
verses are like wounded
fauns seeking refuge in the
forest.

I want to share my fate with
the world's humble. A little
mountain stream pleases me
more than the ocean.

English lyrics

1. I'm just a man who is trying
   to do some good before dying,
   To ask each man and his brother
   To bear no ill toward each other.
   This life will never be hollow -
   To those who listen and follow.

2. I write my rhymes with no learning,
   And yet with truth they are burning,
   But 'is the world waiting for them?
   Or will they all just ignore them?
   Have I a poet's illusion,
   A dream to die in seclusion? (Chorus)

3. A little brook on a mountain,
   The cooling spray of a fountain -
   Arouse in me an emotion, more
   than the vast boundless ocean,
   For there's a wealth beyond measure
   In little things that we treasure.
   (final Chorus, in Spanish)

HIMNO NACIONAL MEXICANO

(MEXICAN NATIONAL HYMN)

Arranged
by
PAUL HILL

Music by JAIME NUNO
Arranged by PAUL HILL

HOW INSENSITIVE

Original Words by VINICIUS DE MORAES
English Words by NORMAN GIMBEL
Music by ANTONIO CARLOS JOBIM

MCA music publishing

IT'S IMPOSSIBLE
(SOMOS NOVIOS)

English Lyric by SID WAYNE
Spanish Words and Music by A. MANZANERO

131

IN A LITTLE SPANISH TOWN

('TWAS ON A NIGHT LIKE THIS)

Words by SAM M. LEWIS and JOE YOUN
Music by MABEL WAYN

Chorus, Slowly with much expression

In A Lit - tle Span - ish Town, 'Twas on a night like this, _____

Stars were peek - a - boo - ing down, 'Twas on a night like this, _____

I whis - pered "Be true to me," _____ And she

sighed: "Si, Si." _____

LA GOLONDRINA

(THE SWALLOW)

English Lyrics by MARJORIE HARPER
Arranged by R. ROSAMOND JOHNSON

136

VERSE

Beloved bird, my fellow pilgrim winging,
  I hear thee singing, as I sang of old!
If it should be,
That thou should come with me,
I shall make for thee,
  A haven from the cold!

CHORUS

Small swallow flying,
The storms of the winter defying,
Where art thou plying?
  Tell me, where dost thou go?
Where'er thou art,
Now I pledge thee my heart,
As this day I part,
  With ev'ry joy I know!

Adonde irá veloz y fatigada
La golondrina que de aqui se vá.
O si en el viento se hallará extraviada
Buscando abrigo y no lo encontrará.
Junto a mi lecho le pondré su nido
En dondo pueda la estación pasar;
Tambien yo estoy en la región perdido
Oh cielo santo! y sin poder volar.

Dejé también mi patria idolatrada,
Esa mansion que me miró nacer,
Mi vida es hoy errante y angustiada
I ya no puedo á mi mansion volver.
Ave querida, amada peregrina,
Mi corazón al tuyo estrecharé,
Oiré tu canto, tierna golondrina,
Recordaré mi patria y lloraré.

KISS OF FIRE

Words and Music by LESTER ALLEN and ROBERT HILL
(Adapted from A.G. VILLOLDO)

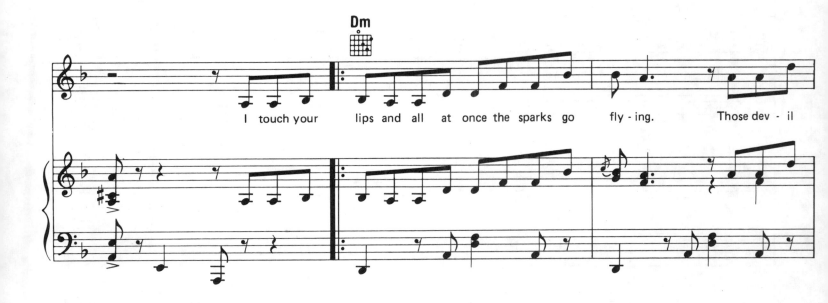

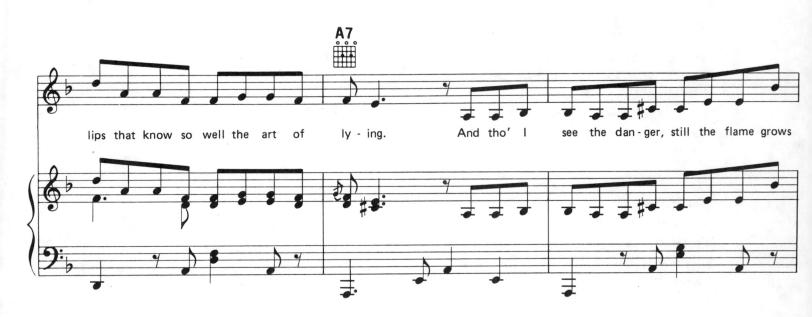

141

LA CUCARACHA

(THE MEXICAN COCKROACH SONG)

English Text by STANLEY ADAMS
Arranged by PAUL HILL

143

4.

La Cucaracha, La Cucaracha,
Woke up on election day,
La Cucaracha, La Cucaracha,
Heard the things they had to say,
A lot of lying and alibing,
Empty heads without a plan,
La Cucaracha, La Cucaracha,
Said, "I'm glad I'm not a man?"

REFRAIN

Then one day he saw an army,
Said,"The drums and bugle charm me,
Still if all the world are brothers,
Why should these men fight the others?
Guess it's just for love and glory,
Who'd believe another story?
These are men so brave and plucky,
Look at me, boy am I lucky!"

5.

La Cucaracha, La Cucaracha,
Wondered where his love could be,
La Cucaracha, La Cucaracha,
Wandered on so mis'rably.
The bees and beetles and old boll weevils,
Chased him off with many "Scats",
First they would scold him and then they told him,
They were bug aristocrats.

REFRAIN

Then one day while in the garden,
He just said, "I beg your pardon",
To a lady Cucaracha,
And he added, "Now I've gotcha."
She was coy but she was willing,
And for years their love was thrilling,
They still meet at half past seven,
Up in Cucaracha heaven.

La Cucaracha, La Cucaracha,
Just the same as you and I,
He got the jitters, the sweets and bitters,
Lived and loved and said "Goodbye."

LA CUMPARSITA

(THE MASKED ONE)

Arranged by
FEDERICO LONGAS

By G. H. MATOS RODRIGUEZ

LA PALOMA

(THE DOVE)

English Lyrics by MARJORIE HARPER
Music by D. DE YRADIER
Arranged by R. ROSAMOND JOHNSON

2.

I'll give you my hand, with all of the love I own;

I'll live all my life for you and you alone;

We'll go to church for blessings that wait in store,

And so - there'll be one where two had been before.

3.

The day we are married, we'll tell the world "Goodbye,"

Away we will go together, you and I.

But when time has passed us by with each coming year,

'Tis then, many little Gauchos will appear.

2.

El dia que nos casemos
  Valgamé Dios!
En la semana que hay ir
  Me hace reir
Desde la Yglesia juntitos
  Que si senor
Nos hiremos a dormir
  Alla voy yó
Si a tu ventana llega etc.

3.

Cuando el curita nos seche
  La bendicion
En la Yglesia Catrédal
  Alla voy yó
Yo te duré la manita
  Con mucho amor
Y el cura dos hisopazos
  Que si senor
Si a tu ventana llega etc.

LAGRIMAS

Words and Music by MANUEL ALEJANDRO
and MARIA ALEJANDRA

Yo sien-to hun-dir - me

y me es - tre - mez - co si

ve - o ca - er _____ tus lá - gri - mas.

Yo me a - rre - pien - to

del mal que_ha-ya he - cho   si

ve - o ca - er___ tus lá - gri - mas. _

Yo te con - sue - lo,   te a -

el len - gua - je mu - do de ___ tu pe - na. Lá -
de pas - sión - es hon - das y ___ de he - ri - das. Lá -

Fm

- gri - mas, la ca - lla - da voz ___ de tu ___
- gri - mas, de do - lor pro - fun ___ do y de a-

Bbm

___ tris - te - za. Lá - gri - mas, la ex - pre -
- le - grí as. Lá - gri - mas, la pa -

Eb7

sión mo - ja - da de ___ tu al - ma. Lá - gri - mas,
la - bra fiel de tu a - mar - gu - ra. Lá - gri - mas,

Repeat and Fade

-gri mas, la ca - lla - da voz __ de tu __ tris te - za. Lá - gri - mas, la ex - pre - sión mo - ja - da de __ tu al - ma. Lá - gri - mas, la vi - si - ble mues - tra de __ que me a - mas. Lá -

LAIA LADAIA
(REZA)

Words and Music by RUY GUERRA and EDU LOBO
English Words by NORMAN GIMBEL

160

162

LAS MAÑANITAS

(GOOD MORNING)

English Lyrics by CAROL RAVEN
Arranged by PAUL HILL

LIKE A LOVER
(O CANTADOR)

Music by DORY CAYMMI and NELSON MOTA
English Lyric by MARILYN and ALAN BERGMAN

LITTLE BOAT

(O BARQUINHO)

Original Words by RONALDO BOSCOLI
English Words by BUDDY KAYE
Music by ROBERTO MENESCAL

Moderately

My lit-tle boat is like____ a note bounc-ing mer-ri-ly a-long, hear it

splash-in' up a song. The sails are white, the sky____ is bright head-in'

LET GO

Original Words by VINICIUS DeMORAES
Music by BADEN POWELL
English Words by NORMAN GIMBEL

You keep what you're feel - ing _____ in - side, _____ all bur - ied and boxed up _____ in - side. _____ The love that you're feel - ing _____ in - side, _____ the pit - y you're feel - ing _____ in - side, _____

MAMÁ INEZ

Words by L. WOLFE GILBERT
Music by ELISEO GRENET

Moderately

In Slop-py Joe's,__ in Hav-an-a a I lin-gered quench-ing my
grace-ful beau-ty and rhy-thm Had nev-er come to my

thirst I saw a danc-er there That was real-ly where
sight She made me want to stay Danced my heart a-way

1.
I saw her first

2.
Such night. Oh Mom-e nez,__
most ev-'ry nez,__

MALAGUEÑA

Music and Spanish Lyric by ERNESTO LECUONA
English Lyric by MARIAN BANKS

Transcription by
GREGORY STONE

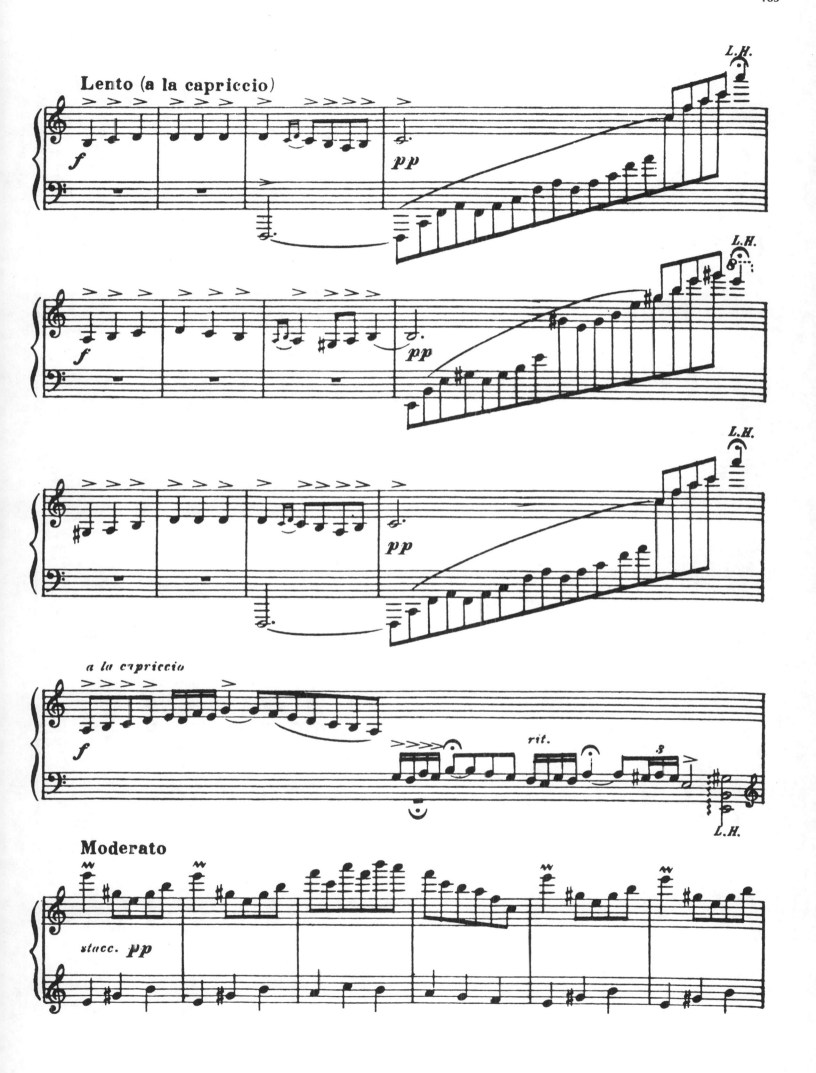

187

MANAGUA, NICARAGUA

Words by ALBERT GAMSE
Music by IRVING FIELDS

190

A DAY IN THE LIFE OF A FOOL
(MANHÃ DE CARNAVAL)

Words by CARL SIGMAN
Music by LUIZ BONFA

Slowly, with a Bossa Nova beat

A day _____ in the life _____ of a fool, _____
Ma - nhã _____ tão bo - ni - ta ma - nhã. _____

_____ a sad _____ and a long, _____ lone - ly
_____ De um di - a fe - liz _____ que che -

day. _____ I walk the av - e - nue
gou. _____ O sol ne céu sur - giu _____

MAÑANA

Words and Music by PEGGY LEE
and DAVE BARBOUR

See additional lyrics

The fau-cet she is drip-ping and the
moth-er's al-ways work-ing; she's

fence she's fall-ing down. My
work-ing ver-y hard. But

pock-et needs some mon-ey so I
ev-'ry time she looks for me I'm

Bb   G7   Cm

ña - na, _____ ma - ña - na, _____

F7

____ ma - ña - na ____ is soon e - nough ___ for

Bb   1-4   F7   5 Bb

me.   My

Additional Lyrics

3. Oh, once I had some money but I gave it to my friend.
   He said he'd pay me double, it was only for a lend.
   But he said a little later that the horse she was so slow.
   Why he gave the horse my money is something I don't know.

4. My brother took his suitcase and he went away to school.
   My father said he only learn'd to be a silly fool.
   My father said that I should learn to make a chili pot.
   But then I burn'd the house down the chili was too hot.

5. The window she is broken and the rain is coming in.
   If someone doesn't fix it I'll be soaking to my skin.
   But if we wait a day or two the rain may go away.
   And we don't need a window on such a sunny day.

MEDITATION

English Words by NORMAN GIMBEL
Original Words by NEWTON MENDONCA
Music by ANTONIO CARLOS JOBIM

Relaxed

mf

C **B7sus** **B7**

In _____ my lone-li-ness _____ When you're gone _____
Though _____ you're far a-way _____ I have on -

C **Em7**

___ and I'm all ___ by my-self ___ and I ___ need your ___ ca-ress. ___
-ly to close ___ my eyes ___ and you ___ are back ___ to stay. ___

A7+5 **Dm7** **Fm7**

___ I _____ just think ___ of you ___
___ I _____ just close ___ my eyes ___

MI SOMBRERO

By AL STILLMAN,
PEDRO BERRIOS and XAVIER CUGAT

204

Additional Lyrics

2. My Sombrero sits upon my head,
Without the aid of pins;
And it covers up, as I have said,
A multitude of sins;
My Sombrero has a nest of birds
On its colossal crown;
And they feel so at home,
On the top of my dome,
That they just refuse to come down.

3. My Sombrero would appear to hail,
From Cuba's sunny shore;
But I bought it at a bargain sale
In a department store.
My Sombrero cost $1.10
With coat and trousers free;
And this outfit I wear
At each evening affair,
And at every afternoon tea.

MEXICAN HAT DANCE
(Jarabe Topatio)

F. A. PARTICHELA
Arranged by J. ROSAMOND JOHNSON

208

MI RIVAL

(MY RIVAL)

English Lyric by ABE TUVIM
Spanish Lyric by MARIA TERESA LARA
Music by MARIA TERESA LARA
Supervision of AUGUSTINE LARA

211

MI VIDA

By ERNESTO LECUONA

MIAMI BEACH RUMBA

Words by ALBERT GAMSE
Music by IRVING FIELDS

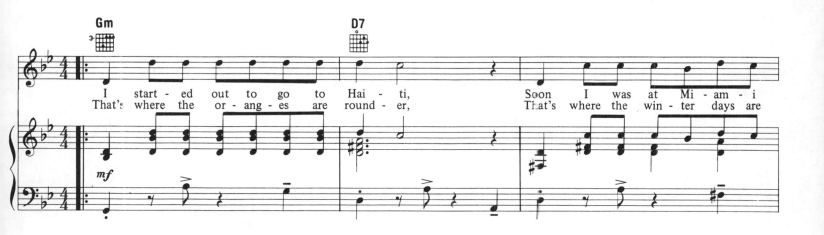

MY SHAWL

English Lyric by STANLEY ADAMS
Spanish Lyric by PEDRO BERRIOS
Music by XAVIER CUGAT

In some Cu - ban town _____ you
A - lla en el ba - tey _____ A -

stop, watch - ing an old ma - ker of shawls, _____ A
lla ba - jo la som - bra de un pal - mar _____ Em -

quaint lit - tle man _____ whose gay col - ored ba
pe - za - ba un rey _____ La fies - ta de su

NEGRA CONSENTIDA

(MY PET BRUNETTE)

English Words by MARJORIE HARPER
Spanish Words and Music by JOAQUIN PARDAVE
Arranged by ELMER SCHOEBET

NOCHE AZUL
(BLUE NIGHT)

English Lyrics by MARJORIE HARPER
Spanish Lyrics by J.S. ESPINOSA DE LOS MONTEROS
Music by CARLOS ESPINOSA DE LOS MONTEROS

Arranged by J. Rosamond Johnson

A. Wagner & Levien   *) Symbols and Diagrams are for Guitar

229

O NOSSO AMOR

(CARNAVAL SAMBA)

Piano Solo

By ANTONIO CARLOS JOBIM

Samba Tempo

Repeat ad lib. - fading out

OBA OBA

By LUIZ BONFA,
TONY JAFFEE and MARIA TOLEDO

ONCE I LOVED

Lyric by RAY GILBERT
Music by ANTONIO CARLOS JOBIM
Portugese Lyric by VINICIUS DeMORAES

ONE NOTE SAMBA

Original Lyrics by NEWTON MENDONCA
English Lyrics by ANTONIO CARLOS JOBIM
Music by ANTONIO CARLOS JOBIM

Lightly, with movement

This is just a lit - tle sam - ba built up - on a sin - gle note.

O - ther notes are bound to fol - low but the root is still that note.

Now the new one is the con - se - quence of the one we've just been through

MCA music publishing

THE PEACOCK

English Lyrics by CAROL RAVEN
Music by ERNESTO LECUONA

Once in a gar-den fash-ioned all of dreams _____ a pea-cock sad-ly clam-ored, loud and long, _____ and

PIEL CANELA

By BOBBY CAPO

POINCIANA
(SONG OF THE TREE)

Words by BUDDY BERNIER
Music by NAT SIMON

THE PEANUT VENDOR
(EL MANISERO)

English Words by MARION SUNSHINE and L. WOLFE GILBERT
Music and Spanish Words by MOISES SIMONS

With a lilt

QUIERO DORMIR CANSADO

Words and Music by MANUEL ALEJANDRO
and ANA MAGDALENA

Quie-ro dor-mir___ can-sa - do   pa - ra no pen-sar   en tí;___
Quie-ro dor-mir___ can-sa - do   y no des-per-tar   ja - más;___

quie-ro dor-mir___ pro-fun - da-men - te
quie-ro dor-mir___ e - ter - na men - te

QUEDATE CONMIGO ESTA NOCHE

Words and Music by
JUAN GABRIEL

QUIET NIGHTS OF QUIET STARS
(CORCOVADO)

English Words by GENE LEES
Original Words & Music by ANTONIO CARLOS JOBIM

Moderately slow

MCA music publishing

SAMBA DE ORFEU

Words by ANTONIO MARIA
Music by LUIZ BONFA

SAY "SI, SI"

Music by ERNESTO LECUONA
Spanish Words by FRANCIA LUBAN
English Words by AL STILLMAN

Here's a lit-tle know-ledge ____
Va - mos a la con - ga ____

quite good. ____
Ay *Dios* ____

May-be it won't
Va - mos qe ya

Spain they _ say _____ "Si, Si;" _____
Hin - du - stan _____ "Ug, Ug;" _____
ra   Vi - go _____ *me   voy* _____

_ In France you'll _ hear _____ "Wee,
_ Means "O. K., _ babe, _ let's
_ *Mi   ne - gra _ di* _____ *me   a*

Wee;" _____
hug." _____
dios _____
                                        Ev - 'ry lit - tle Dutch girl _ says_
                                        Nev - er was a Pan - a - ma_
                                        An - da   bon - go - se - ro_ to -

no chord

Additional Lyrics

3. The monkeys in the tree
Don't have to say: "Si, Si";
All they do is wag their little tails;
That's a little gag that never fails.
In darkest Africa
The natives say; "Uh, Huh!"
But you never hear my plea,
Won't say "Yes" in any language to me.
When will you say:"Si, Si"?

4. Out West they say: "Wah Hoo!"
That's "O.K., Toots" to you.
Every Southern lady knows her stuff,
'Cause her answer always is "Sho Nuff!"
But, sweetheart, tell me why,
No matter how I try,
You won't listen to my plea,
Won't say "Yes" in any language to me.
When will you say:"Si, Si"?

5. In Washington, D.C.,
The yes-men say: "Si, Si";
There are lots of politicians, though
Who can always say both "Yes" and "No".
But sweetheart tell me why,
No matter how I try,
You won't listen to my plea,
Won't say "Yes" in any language to me.
When will you say:"Si, Si"?

6. A lady horse, they say,
Means "Yes" when she says: "Neigh!"
Every little gal from Mexico
Hates to give a pal a "No, No, No!"
So, sweetheart, tell me why,
No matter how I try,
You won't listen to my plea,
Won't say "Yes" in any language to me.
When will you say:"Si, Si"?

7. In 606 B.C.,
Those gals would mix, Si, Si!
Every little cave man used his dome,
Hit 'em on the head, then dragged 'em home.
So, sweetheart, tell me why,
No matter how I try,
You won't listen to my plea,
Won't say "Yes" in any language to me.
When will you say:"Si, Si"?

SHE'S A CARIOCA

Lyric by RAY GILBERT
Music by ANTONIO CARLOS JOBIM
Portugese Lyric by VINICIUS deMORAES

SIX LESSONS
FROM MADAME LA ZONGA

Lyric by CHARLES NEWMAN
Music by JAMES V. MONACO

SIMILAU
(SEE-ME-LO)

Words by HARRY COLEMAN
Music by ARDEN CLAR

Moderately

Spir - it in de wood beat de hol - low cane.
Spir - it in de heart make de blood flow fast.

Spir - it in de wood float a -
Spir - it in de heart make de

way de pain.
mus - cle last.

Make de bod - y ripe and a - live a - gain.
Keep de hope a - live when de youth go past.

Ay, Sim - i -

lau. _____

When de wom-an come up - on de scene_

SO NICE

(SUMMER SAMBA)

Relaxed Bossa Nova

Original Words and Music by MARCOS VALLE and PAULO SERGIO VALLE
English Words by NORMAN GIMBEL

Some-one to hold me tight, that would be ver-y nice Some-one to love me right, that would be ver-y nice. Some-one to un-der-stand each lit-tle dream __ in me, some-one to take my hand, to be a team __ with me. So nice, _____

SOMEONE TO LIGHT UP MY LIFE
(SE TODOS FOSSEM IGUAIS A VOCE)

English Lyric by GENE LEES
Original text by VINICIUS de MORAES
Music by ANTONIO CARLOS JOBIM

SONG OF THE JET

(SAMBA DO AVIAO)
(From The Film "COPACABANA PALACE")

English lyric by GENE LEES
Original Text and Music by ANTONIO CARLOS JOBIM

Moderate Bossa Nova

SOUTH OF THE BORDER
(DOWN MEXICO WAY)

By JIMMY KENNEDY
and MICHAEL CARR

TANGO OF ROSES

Words by MARJORIE HARPER
Music by VITTORIO MASCHERONI

Moderate Tango

See how red the ros - es grow, As though they try to show the ve - ry fi - re, The same de - sire, that you in - spire when you ap - pear. Ros - es re - flect my glad - ness, They share my sad - ness when you're not near. They are the em - blems of

VAYA CON DIOS
(MAY GOD BE WITH YOU)

Words and Music by LARRY RUSSELL,
INEZ JAMES & BUDDY PEPPER

WHAT A DIFF'RENCE A DAY MADE

Lyric by STANLEY ADAMS
Music by MARIA GREVER

YELLOW DAYS

English lyric by ALAN BERNSTEIN
Music and Spanish lyric by ALVARO CARRILLO

With An Easy Flow

YOURS
(Quiereme Mucho)

Words by ALBERT GAMSE and JACK SHERR
Music by GONZALO ROIG

ZACATECAS
(MEXICAN MARCH)

By H. GENARO CODINA
New Edition by JACOB M. VELT

YESTERDAY I HEARD THE RAIN
(ESTA TARDE VI LLOVER)

By ARMANDO MANZANERO
English Lyrics by GENE LEES